MARCH 18, 2003

Michael Lally

MARCH 18, 2003

a poem for peace

Drawings by ALEX KATZ

Libellum

CHARTA

A Preface to Michael Lally

Vincent Katz

Who needs no preface. Michael is one of those guys who's been on the scene since you were in pigtails. I've known his work since I was a teenager and he was suave, debonair, edgy, but always cool with kids. When I began reading his poems, I began to learn something about him, since he seemed to lay it all on the line in his poems of the 1970s, a seeming synthesis of Ginsberg's and O'Hara's different personal politics. I gleaned that he came from a street-fighting part of New Jersey, liked black girls, and later, guys. Poems like "In Harlem In 1961" set the tone:

> i didn't think about it
> i was in harlem with you
> it was 1961 and we were
> alone, in love, uptown,
> way uptown on a hundred
> and thirty something street
> heading downtown where
> people didn't stare.....

But I always knew, too, that Michael went beyond the limitations of "influence," or "scene," that he was voracious, and that applied to literature as well as to life, and that anyone with intelligence and appetite who reads that much takes it in, and it makes her or him a more sophisticated entity.

Then Michael moved to L.A. He'd had enough of New York, of the changing neighborhood, of being only a poet. He was an actor and went to do it in the city of angels. He stayed and worked there, but just as earlier he had tried a life as jazz piano player, he finally found that life as actor was also an extra thing, extra to being a poet, which is what he truly was and is. He began to take more stock of his poetry. He began publishing more, with presses such as Coffee House and Black Sparrow. He consolidated his position as a major voice. What helped hook audiences into his history, which is a living, not a closed, history, were his memoirs, which he began publishing in books in conjunction with poetry. *It's Not Nostalgia* (1999) and *It Takes One To Know One* (2001) are stunning personal testaments. We learn about the person, at the same time as we are entertained by the luminousness of his writing. Lally is so street that he can wear that power lightly.

Through the poetry and the prose, we learn how Lally was in the U.S. air force in the early 1960s, happened to see Frank O'Hara's book *Lunch Poems* on a table in a friend's apartment, at first rejected any idea of poetry, then opened it and found "The Day Lady Died," O'Hara's timeless elegy for Billie Holiday, and was transformed. His life was saved that day. We also learn of his later political activism, how he organized protests against the Vietnam War and was almost elected sheriff of a county in Iowa, running on the Peace and Freedom ticket, how he was transformed, over and over, by the movements of the time, not "movement" in the sense of something you hear about and then go sign up for, but movement as a great tidal wave sweeping a nation or continent. Lally's open bi-sexuality was one aspect of his involvement with gay liberation, black liberation, women's liberation.

Fast forward to 9/11. Ever since that fateful day, the United States has been in a downward spiral. Whoever was behind those events — and I do not feel at all confident I know who was — achieved the results they desired: the country and the world have become acutely polarized. To say that civil liberties have been curtailed is a tragic understatement. As constitutional expert *par excellence* Laurence Tribe stated in a recent lecture, the U.S. constitution is in grave danger. Checks and balances are being thrown by the wayside; centralized power is being allowed to reign unchecked. Former Supreme Court Justice Sandra Day O'Connor, of all conservative people, has said that the United States is on the path to dictatorship. Quoting from Nina Totenberg's report of O'Connor's speech, "It takes a lot of degeneration before a country falls into dictatorship, she said, but we should avoid these ends by avoiding these beginnings" (NPR, 3/10/06).

So many beginnings too, we have in fighting injustice. In "March 18, 2003," Lally asks,

> In the past, wasn't the vast right-wing conspiracy
> always on the wrong side of history—
> *for* the king, *against* the revolution,
> *for* slavery, *against* the eight-hour day,
> *for* child labor and Jim Crow segregation,
> *against* votes for women,
> *for* legal discrimination, *against* immigrants
> and Catholics, Hispanics and African Americans,
> *for* treating corporations like privileged
> individuals, and individuals like
> corporate privileges?

His razor-sharp delineations strike home, but they also strike a chord. They are not as an arrow flying blindly into the night; they work, because they resonate with other tonalities, particular American tonalities. We Americans do not have to lower our heads in shame. *We* did not go to war in Vietnam, and *we* did not give the president the power to make war at his whim in the fall of 2001. *We* do contain multitudes, and *we* contain some of the most powerful voices for justice, and for a democratic vision.

> Great is Justice;
> Justice is not settled by legislators and laws . . . . it is in the soul,
> It cannot be varied by statutes any more than love or pride or the
>   attraction of gravity can,
> It is immutable . . it does not depend on majorities . . . . majorities or
> what not come at last before the same passionless and exact tribunal.

These lines from the end of Walt Whitman's contrarian epic, *Leaves Of Grass*, strike notes that we find often in American thought and literature — from Thoreau and Emerson, through Sandburg and Sinclair, Malcolm X, and numerous other women and men, poets and thinkers, to the present day. Like Whitman, Sandburg grew up working — a theater sceneshifter, potter, dishwasher — and he too wrote a democratic epic, called *The People, Yes*. In it, he skewers popular misconceptions, writing:

> The people having nothing to lose take chances.
> The people having nothing to take care of are careless.
> The people lacking property are slack about property.
> Having no taxes to pay how can they consider taxes?
> "And the poor have they not themselves to blame for their poverty?"

Lally's new poem enters into this tradition, which is also the tradition of Woody Guthrie and Bob Dylan, and he enters it at a particularly precipitous moment in human history. With one nation at such a great advantage in wealth and military might over the others, there is the real danger of those in power in that nation losing touch with reality. They have admitted as much, when a government representative told a reporter, in effect, we (the government) change reality; it's your job to find out what we've done. There is a sense of entitlement, a sense of impunity, that has conditioned those in command over the past five years to act with blatant disregard for the law, not to mention common sense or morality.

Lally's poem was written for a specific occasion, an anti-war poetry reading I organized in 2003. Beginning immediately after 9/11, the press, the *New York Times* in particular, picked up the drumbeat of war. It began with scared shouts of "Anthrax! Bomb threats!" And we saw that acquiescence, felt its heat burning the newspaper pages every day. I wanted to get away from that; fortunately, I had the opportunity to go to Italy, to spend a year in Rome then, and I availed myself of other outlets. While in Rome, I read *Il Manifesto*, a sophisticated, intellectual newspaper, with a point of view I could actually respect. In late 2002 and early 2003, the American drumbeat increased to a roar, and the *New York Times* went along for the ride. It took a very long time, until long after the invasion, the declared end of major operations, and subsequent months of daily carnage and dysfunction, for the op-ed pages of the *Times* to begin to criticize the president, which they now do regularly. The front pages, in a much more subtle way, still toe the official line.

In early 2003, I was feeling an acute sense of powerlessness, knowing that the world was being dragged into a war that would cause untold devastation for reasons that were specious. I decided to organize a reading, VERSUS: Poets Against The War, which took place March 18, 2003, at Paula Cooper Gallery in New York. The readers were Ann Lauterbach, Anne Waldman, Michael Lally and Robert Creeley. Ramsay Clark, former

U.S. Attorney General, under Lyndon Johnson, also spoke. All the readers were powerful. Lally's poem had a great impact, partially because it was written specifically for the occasion, addressing the current fears and sense of dread most of us then shared. Knowing Lally's background in politics, coupled with his savoir-faire and poetic skills, I thought he might create some poetic dynamite we could throw at the hate and war mongers. I'm still surprised by the way he came through.

It's hard not to be affected by this poem. Taking the simple rhetorical form of a series of questions, some inane, others brutally pointed, Lally navigates vast seas of emotional and political upset. His vessel is his knowledge of human nature and politics, his sail his belief in the basic goodness of humanity. "March 18, 2003" is not a pessimistic poem. It is realistic but harbors within it the hope that decency can prevail. As it turned out, the United States invaded Iraq the day after the VERSUS reading, etching the poem's title into history's annals of infamy. I decided to publish "March 18, 2003" as the first book in my Libellum imprint; I wanted to get the poem out, and I also wanted to set a tone to which future publications might resonate. I am very happy that Giuseppe Liverani decided we should do a second edition, a collaboration between Charta and Libellum, a reaching of hands across the waters in aesthetic pursuit. For the first edition, Alex Katz did the cover image of two boys embracing. For this edition, he has added five new drawings, made specifically to go with the poem.

Lally's youthful optimism can be observed in another poem, written on a happier occasion, the marriage of his son:

> And in your faces we can read our love's intentions—
> to be true, to be honest and honorable,

to be light and awesome rendering of love's affections
and desires,
to inspire all of us with your delight in each other's company,
to accompany us on our journey into what our hearts might sing
if this were ways to ring our days with your example,
to never trample on the secret sharings of want and
earnest leisure,
the pleasure of your solidarity—

Ultimately, it is that solidarity Lally leaves us with, the belief that things can be better, it doesn't all have to be so venal and hateful. There is space for love and sharing in this world, before it's too late.

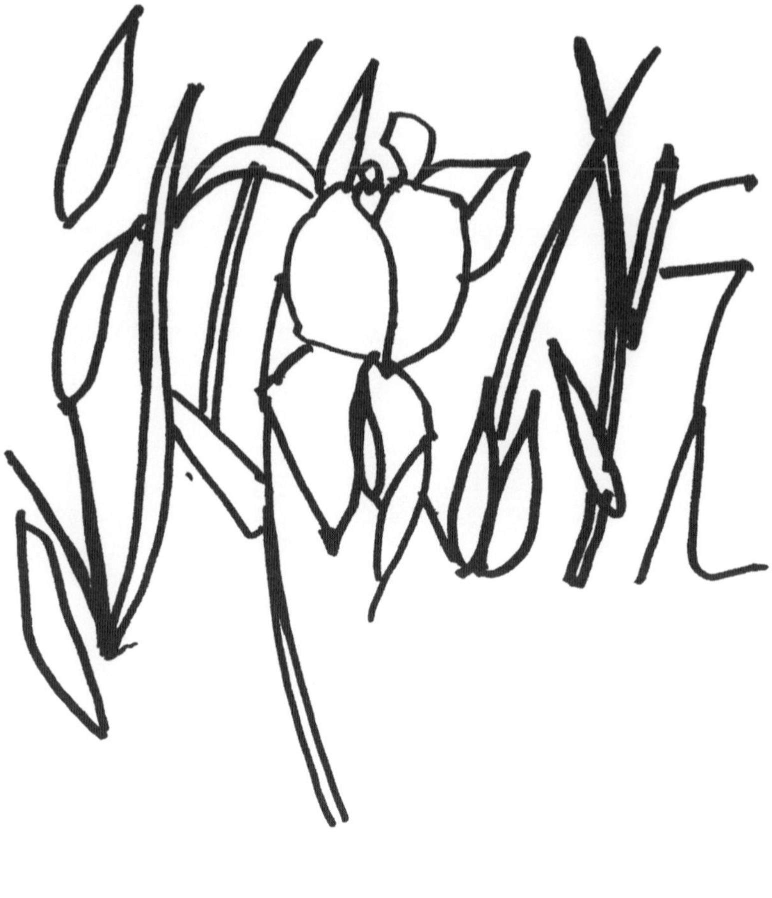

March 18, 2003

I don't have any answers,
just some questions:
Who's gonna win the Oscar for best actor?
Was Bush sedated at that press conference?
When innocent people die is it worse
than when the guilty do?
Guilty of what?
Can you define dry drunk?
Are you as tired as I am
of these right-wing fundamentalists
trying to reverse what little progress
we've managed to make in our attempts
to create, as Che once said, a world
where love is more possible?
Are some kids more precious than others?
If some white folks build
a housing complex on an Indian reservation

with money from white supremacists
and they use the few resources
the reservation has to make their housing project
bigger and better than the Native American houses
and some of the Native Americans
demonstrate against this, and the response
of our government is to build a barbed wire fence
around the white enclave and send soldiers
to man watchtowers and protect the whites
and this pisses the Native Americans off
and their demonstrations get rowdy
and some Indian kids throw rocks at the soldiers
and the soldiers shoot and kill some of these kids
and the Indians get even more upset
and vow to stop the settlements
and get the whites off their land
and some try and fight but to no avail
since their weapons are no match for the overwhelming power
of our government forces and this
only makes the Indians madder
and our government sends in more soldiers

with tanks and armor and builds more settlements
for more white people and then an Indian comes up
with a way to build a bomb that you have to be willing
to kill yourself to detonate and a young Indian volunteers
and blows himself up along with some innocent whites
including children and the response of our government is to
bulldoze into oblivion the house of his family
and some of their neighbors' houses too and
a pregnant young Indian woman is crushed by a falling wall
because the soldiers told her family to stay inside
and then the soldiers take over the reservation
and won't let the Indians go out to get food
or go to work and if they do go out during curfew
some of them are shot and killed—who
would be the innocent ones in all that
—and the guilty?
Is that question anti-Semitic?
What's gonna win the Oscar for best picture?
Do you have to have Irish ancestors
who came over around the time of
Gangs of New York to leave that film not

dismissive of the dumbed down Hollywood plot
or the mostly inappropriate Hollywood casting
but instead overwhelmed with shock and
rage and a deep inarticulate sadness?
Do my relatives in uniform support Bush
because the right-wing fundamentalists
are really that good at manipulating the media
a media mostly owned by them
but which they continue to attack as liberal
in order to debunk any questioning of their tactics
and actions by the small percentage
of media outlets that are halfway independent of them?
You call this a poem?
Are the Arabs to blame for their problems?
Are Native Americans?
Are Irish Catholics in Northern Ireland?
Are the Tutus? The North Koreans?
Patty Hearst? Muhammad Ali?
Chris Reeves? The Jews? The Tibetans?
Southern Baptists? Hollywood?
Wall Street? Enron? Ford? Mariah Carey?

Crispin Glover? The Catholic priesthood?
The Chechens? The Colombians?
The troops in Kuwait and Iraq?
Are we?
What makes me think I can wait till the last minute
to write a poem about how humbled
I am by the idea
that poetry can do anything to stop
the carnage anywhere—except in our hearts
however briefly?
Wasn't I the only veteran on the stage,
the night in 1966 when I took part in my first
anti-war poetry reading?
If Bush wins in Iraq and Osama is caught and
the economy rebounds enough to give people
some hope is his re-election inevitable?
Is it inevitable anyway?
Should those who voted for Nader be forced
to apologize to the innocent victims of Bush's policies?
Or for his renewed attack on the environment
in the hypocritical but seemingly successful guise

of a man who actually cares about clean air?
Why are Democrats who are smart enough and
tough enough and good enough politicians to play hard ball
with the right-wing pricks so rare?
Do we only care about war
and the innocent lives it takes
when Americans are at risk?
Isn't it obvious that wars never end,
they just move?
What good did our pointing out that Malcolm X
and Martin Luther King were only assassinated
after they stopped talking about race and began
talking about class and the rights of poor people do?
Isn't it obvious these right-wing fundamentalists
are still pissed off about what FDR did for working folk
with social security and tried to do with health care
and other programs that they've since managed to
dismantle or are still attempting to? Isn't it ironic
how much they hate Carter for being a true Christian
and showing them up for the hypocrites they are?
Do these right-wing fundamentalists really believe

that the founding fathers were born-again Christians
who believe, like Bush, that only they'll go to heaven
when "the rapture" comes,
when the framers of the constitution
barely believed in organized religion
and none took the Bible literally?
If the right-wing fundamentalists
really believe we should all follow the Bible's
directions, why wasn't Newt Gingrich
buried in sand up to his neck and stoned to death
when he cheated on his first wife with his second
and then on his second with his third?
Can you get more hypocritical than to try and impeach
a president for adulterous sex with an intern
when you are doing the same exact thing
at the same exact time?
Is it true even Newt thinks this attack on Iraq is ill conceived?
Ever notice how much Bush Junior
looks like his cousin Prince Charles,
with the same shaped faces and big ears
and those long straight noses and beady eyes,

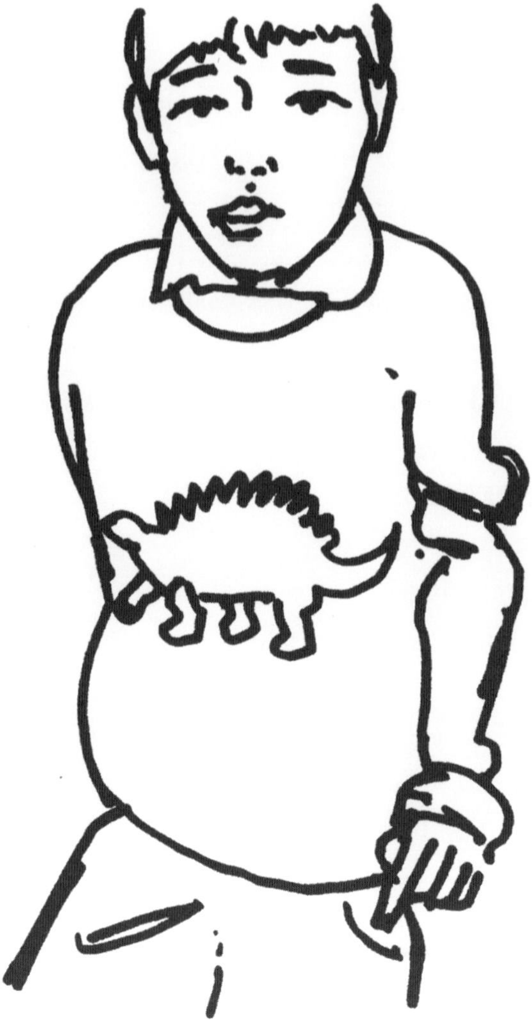

and thin-lipped superior smirks, though Charles
is better trained to hide his?
Is it any wonder Junior acts like he rules
by divine right—when he obviously does?
Isn't it as though the American Revolution
has been reversed without a fight?
Has the vast right-wing conspiracy triumphed
at last—with an almost complete takeover
by an alcoholic spoiled brat with
a right-wing Christian fundamentalist makeover?
Isn't their "good and evil"
"you're either with us or against us" thing—
like a drink to a dry drunk
on an imperial binge?
In the past, wasn't the vast right-wing conspiracy
always on the wrong side of history—
for the king, *against* the revolution,
for slavery, *against* the eight-hour day,
for child labor and Jim Crow segregation,
against votes for women,
for legal discrimination, *against* immigrants

and Catholics, Hispanics and African Americans,
for treating corporations like privileged
individuals, and individuals like
corporate privileges?
Or is history still on their
side with that one, as corporate power
grows and equality slows, at least the kind
based on the chance to make a living?
Isn't it true that during the fabulous
fucked-up fifties they pretend to be
so nostalgic for, they ignore the part
about how ordinary citizens won the war
and came home to a nation tired of
depression and built unions strong enough
to give a working man a chance to
own a home and keep up with the Joneses
if not the Walkers and Bushes?
Wasn't the difference between liberal capitalists
and conservative capitalists summed up best
by JFK's old man during the Depression—
when he said he was willing to give up half of what he had

to keep the other half while
the conservatives aren't
willing to give up anything?
Wasn't the first thing they protected after 9/11
offshore banking and headquarters for corporations
and wealthy individuals to avoid paying the taxes
the rest of us do even if that's how and where
the terrorists and drug barons hide their money too?
Wasn't the next thing they bailed out the airlines
because of all the fuel they use and anything that
helps make unconscionable profits for oil companies
is their first priority?
Isn't it true their oil corporate patrons wanted to run
a pipeline through Afghanistan but the Taliban
wouldn't let them and now
the new Afghan government will?
Didn't the CIA overthrow
the democratically elected leader of Iran in 1953
with the help of a Nazi collaborator
who immediately set up 25-year leases
on Iran's oil for three U.S. firms including Gulf Oil?

Didn't Kermit Roosevelt, the CIA head of that region,
retire shortly thereafter to a
vice presidency of—Gulf Oil?
Didn't the CIA back the coup
that overthrew the democratically elected
president of 1950s Guatemala because of his proposal
to nationalize some of United Fruit's vast holdings?
Didn't Walter Bedell Smith,
the CIA man in charge, within a year
become a member of the board of directors
of—you guessed it—The United Fruit Company?
Does anyone see echoes of that today
in Cheney's connections to Halliburton
or Bush's to Enron?
Isn't it true that this shit has been going on forever?
Isn't it also true that our government,
which usually means one of the secret agencies
with secret funding for which the constitution
never allowed,
trained and paid the leaders of al-Qaeda
in the Afghan proxy war with the Soviets

as well as supplied the necessary
ingredients for Saddam's weapons
of mass destruction including the gas he used
against the Kurds and the helicopters to transport it
and that Bush and his cohorts including his wife
never mentioned the ways the Taliban oppressed women
or Saddam killed his own people until it was convenient politically
and still don't talk about how daddy's cohorts and business
partners in Saudi Arabia have links to Osama and his movement
and oppress women and all the other atrocities
dictatorships and oligarchies have been committing
with our government's blessings
throughout our history?
You call this poetry?
When Bush senior offered to get rid of
America's chemical arsenal, didn't he mean
only the already old and leaking and
no longer feasible ones the U.S. had stockpiled
and not the new improved and even
deadlier ones it kept on making?
Don't the links between the CIA and

drug smuggling date back to its beginnings?
In fact, can't you track which country the CIA is trying
to get something from or do something to
by which drug is the latest "epidemic"?
Hasn't the killing of innocent civilians
always been a tactic in war, from Biblical times
through Dresden and Hiroshima to Vietnam and
El Salvador, or Kosovo and the Congo?
Aren't we all gonna die?
Are we obsessed with the denial of that reality?
As a kid did you, like I, feel
you owned death, like a furry little pet
sitting on your shoulder, and any time you wanted
you could turn your head and see it, or kiss it,
or pet it, or remind yourself how close it was,
but in truth, you thought of it rarely,
more frequently of everyone else's,
because theirs seemed more imminent
even though back then you felt it
breathing on your neck in reassurance?
Or is that just me because I've seen

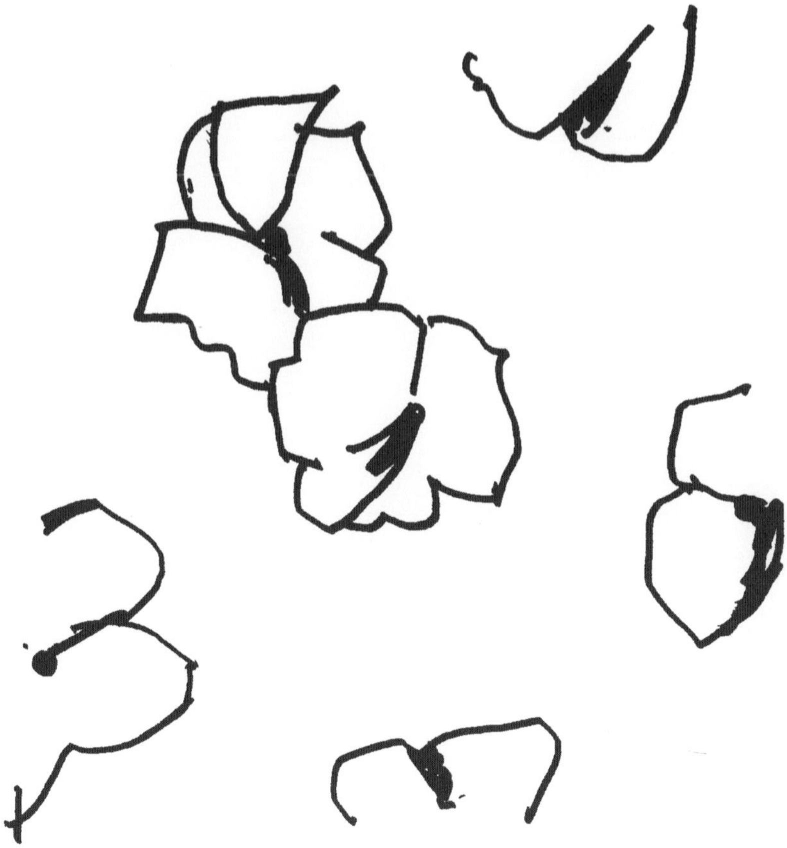

a lot of people pass, or die, as you might say,
from one thing or another, including my mother
in a way that seemed unfair and certainly
unnecessary and arbitrary and cruel?
But what death isn't?
Those I remember that were no surprise,
though devastating anyway in their
now-you-see-me
now-you-never-will-again
finality?
Is that why now it's life I'm obsessed with?
Or is that because when I watched
the second plane crash into the second tower on TV
a thin blue tube hung from my urethra,
attached to a clear plastic bag, the remnant of a
cancer operation the week before,
unaware an old friend was on that flight,
at that moment incinerated,
a woman who was kind to me when
she didn't need to be?
How many people have died

before you got the chance to tell them what you meant to?
Does it seem there's
not enough
sometimes because it is
too much?
Haven't I said and written more than once
that poetry saved my life?
Did it for you?
Wasn't it the only thing that could stop the war
in my heart and head
over where I thought I was being led
by the clan and neighborhood
and extended family of cops
I was born into at the beginning of another war
when the prognosis was bleak for *our* side?
And when the tide turned and with it went
the country's great depression,
didn't that war save us from ourselves,
create a new economy—and ways to milk it?
Didn't my oldest brothers join the service out of
high school, before it was all over,

though it's never all over, as the newsreels
and *Life* magazine made clear to even
my developing child's perception?
But isn't our part in it often hidden,
until later events like those in Korea
drag us in in ways even civilians can't ignore?
Didn't my other brother get drafted
during that war?
But didn't the only one of our clan
who saw real combat, my favorite cousin,
Jackie, always have a joke to make you grin
until I pestered him to let me in
on what war was like up close and he
kept putting me off until he'd had enough
then spat out how he was scared
his whole time there
and when he faced the enemy
he shot into the air, like he was sure they did too,
then got as far from them as he could?
Is that why they don't have the draft anymore?
Is it because I didn't want to have my

boyhood fantasies destroyed, that I convinced myself
he was just kidding again, sparing me
the gory details?
Decades later didn't scholars of war
research Korean battlefields and
determine by the angle of the bullets
they found buried in the ground that most rounds
had to have been fired into the air?
Do we really care who wins a little gold statuette
in La La Land, especially this year?
Not long after the Korean war ended,
wasn't I one of a street corner doo-wop quartet
of pale-faced budding Irish alcoholics
called the Four Roses?
And didn't redheaded Moose Conlon,
the youngest but biggest, later
step on a mine in Viet Nam?
Isn't that his name on a boulder in the park
in the Jersey town where we played ball
when we weren't singing?
Isn't it true the world hasn't been easy for a long time?

Wasn't it once?
Weren't there kids—little
girls in dresses with
skinny legs and bare arms—
and boys too shy to make
as much noise as the others—
under street lamps—out
late, because it's too warm
to go to bed yet—and
nothing good for kids on
the radio anyway—
and nobody really afraid of
anything too strange and
disturbing to threaten their
hopes for more evenings like
this?
Wasn't
the world easy
once?
Wasn't that because we didn't know
and maybe didn't want to

like my nephews and nieces don't
today, as they sail away to foreign ports
called up in the reserves or on the active duty
they see as a way out of the confusion
of a working class that thinks it isn't,
or that class doesn't matter, at least not on
the talk radio they listen to?
Is there no other way for them to go?
Isn't that all they know
despite my talks and books and e-mails?
Don't they say it worked for me,
it's how I first got out into the world?
When I try to tell them why they're wrong
to believe their leaders and the right-wing
corporate radio pimps, isn't it difficult for them to
see, as it was for me, when I used the GI Bill
to attend a university that filled my head with information
that made me dizzy, made me feel crazy,
made me feel alienated from all I'd known
and grown to love the further away
I got from it?

Shit, why didn't anybody tell us
when we beat the lousy Krauts
and stinkin' Japs that the man who
would later get us to the moon, Wernher von Braun,
was the same Nazi scientist who made
the rockets that rained down death on London?
Did any poem of Dylan Thomas ever tell me that?
Who knew the Volkswagen beetle
that the college kids and later lefties
would embrace was Hitler's idea?
Did anyone ever discuss how we obliterated
Dresden, for no strategic reason, or caused
more civilian death and devastation there and
in the fire bombing of Tokyo than with
the atom bombs we dropped?
Why didn't I know that General Electric
got off with a fine and hand slaps
for colluding with the Nazis or that IBM set up
the Nazi's record keeping or that we refused
to bomb the railroad tracks that carried the
freight cars full of Jews to their destination?

Can we guess why our bombs never touched
the Krupp arms factory?
Is it because it isn't
freedom or democracy we fight for or defend,
but in the end its weapons, fuel and drugs—
the trinity that underpins the wealth of nations
and the corporations that rule them?
Did you know the company that makes
the new computerized voting machines
that defied the exit polls and put right-wing
Republicans in power where they weren't before
are owned by the right-wing Republican Senator
who did just that in Nebraska, where
according to the results even a majority of blacks
who said they voted against him were obviously wrong
and did the opposite according to his computers?
Is that why the networks
won't use their own exit polls anymore,
so as not to contradict machines
that leave no inconvenient paper trail
that can be verified,

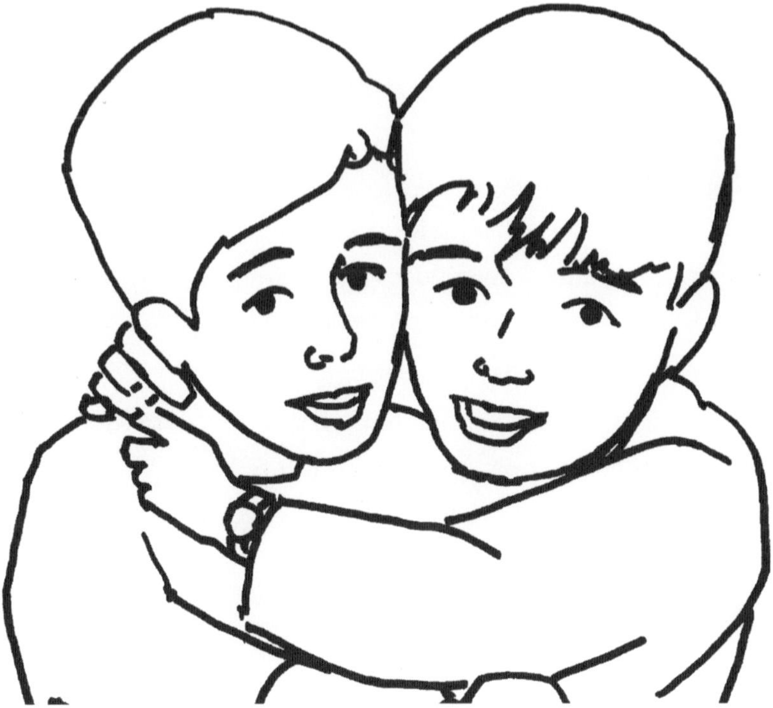

no tabs and chads and all the rest
that almost gave us who we really voted for?
Why would my relatives, in uniform or not,
want to know that,
stifling in the embrace of a fate
much bigger than any whim of Bush the Great
as he seems to see himself?
And why shouldn't he?
Didn't he grow up with the kind of privileges
our families couldn't even guess at?
When I went AWOL for a two week unplanned
vacation in San Francisco of 1962,
didn't I come back to a court martial and its consequences?
When he failed to show for weekend duty
in the Texas National Guard during Viet Nam
for an entire year, didn't he get the same pass
he got when reporters let him gas about
how DUIs at forty are just youthful
indiscretions, not the job losing experiences
they might be for you or me or our families?
But, he never had a job to lose, did he?

Weren't they just favors from his father's friends?
And even when he lost them, didn't somebody else pay
the price, as we are doing now, this night,
especially those paid peanuts to fight
in his place once again?
But is it a whim, or divine right
in his sight, as he's implied?
Have you noticed how
he never mangles his speech when he talks about
bending others to his will, about killing prisoners
in Texas on death row or blowing those he's
designated evil to kingdom come?
Can you see that he's not
dumb, just not a very good liar, stumbling
over words meant to convey compassion or
all the things he knows aren't true?
Wasn't it odd when he
defended himself at his recent news conference
by explaining with exasperation that his
reason for waging war on Iraq was because,
as he emotionally explained, as though

to remedial students, he put his hand
on a Bible and took an oath to defend
the constitution of the United States
of America?
Has Saddam got plans for
destroying our constitution?
Would that be by enticing Bush into an alliance-
breaking terrorist-inciting preemptive
attack on a large source of oil?
Is that too glib?
When American troops found al-Qaeda
training videos in Afghanistan, weren't they
right to be incensed at the tactics being practiced by
these Moslem boys and men against pretend
hostages they might take in an assault on
Ohio or Dubuque—as the trainees screamed
and punched and kicked their innocent victim manqués—
just like the Afghan taxi driver said was
done to him by American women and men
interrogating him about things he had
no knowledge of while chained to

the ceiling and floor like some *New Yorker* cartoon
that isn't funny any more?
Wasn't it the blows and kicks meted out
by an American female that made the Afghan cry,
the humiliation of it as he pissed his pants and
cowered under the physical and verbal abuse
for no more reason, he claimed, than that he
drove his taxi into the wrong street at the
obviously wrong time?
Didn't he also cry at the memory of the
Afghan boys who died in the custody of our interrogators,
never having been away from their
families and homes before their being chained
to ceiling and floor at ankle and wrist while
being deprived of sleep and screamed at
in an English they couldn't decipher?
Didn't the military doctors who did their autopsies
with the same efficient record keeping
that the Nazis perfected say they died of internal injuries?
Am I saying
the gang who tried to permanently eliminate Jews

and Gypsies and queers and the retarded and
deformed and more is what our troops and
their commanders replicate in our name?
Or am I saying war brings out the best and
worst of—but haven't you heard all that before?
Aren't your souls and hearts as sore as mine
from all the confusion and obfuscation and distortion
and repulsion of what others do to others
in the name of having been done to us?
Didn't our government use the same tactics it
deplores Saddam for?
Didn't we try to be honest?
But didn't the truth keep changing on us?
When I was a kid, didn't they teach us that
"Uncle Joe Stalin" helped us win the war?
When I was a man, didn't
Ronald Reagan remember scenes from
war movies as if they really happened
and he was there though he was in Hollywood
the entire time making movies he remembered
as reality?

In the light of his later disease
don't we understand that?
Don't we understand everything, sometimes—
or once?
Is this the way we count the time to go
to get to where we know it will be all right for us again?
Or have we walked through the door to the future
and found ourselves on fire before we can see
the flames and what remains and what must go
is all these fools are fighting over when they pose
as people-in-the-know on where we all have been
and might be going?
Does it matter where we are or the color
of our skin or religion of our ancestors or is that
incidental because what's fundamental about these times
is the way the long hot Summer starts in Winter
one unexpected day and then, say, turns up in Spring
for more than a week, or peaks in Fall
when all we want is a breath of fresh crisp air,
the kind we find some mornings in the mountains
or the North but not as many as before,

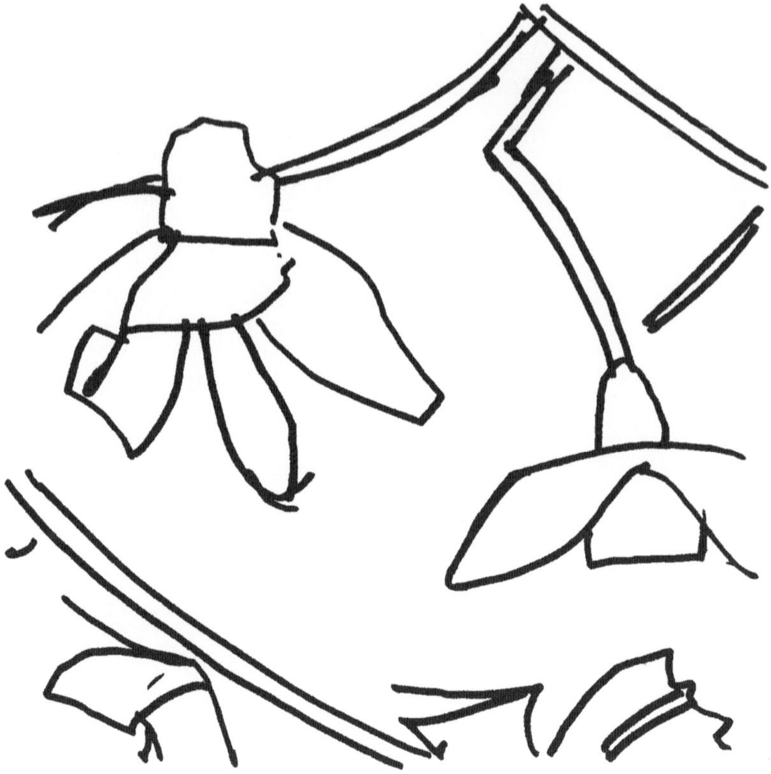

before the earth became a living/dying litmus test
of our deceit in dealing with these tired times
when even trees are gasping to survive
and they're the ones who keep *us* alive?
How much does the changing weather patterns
over Afghanistan that caused the years of drought
that impoverished the country that embraced a Taliban
solution to their problems have to do with lives lost
and the other costs of 9/11?
What legacy do we end with?
Too many CDs and DVDs and not enough
of what it takes to keep us all from baking in the long
hot Summer of a race's demise despite the seemingly
old fashioned Winter we've just survived?
Is it a surprise, that the fate we share is in the air
not in the eyes of some tenacious politician
who pretends he's one of us?
Was Duchamp correct when he said, only in French,
"Tools that are no good require more skill"?
Isn't it too noisy these days?
Can you hear yourself think

with all these hard surfaces
reflecting the clatter
of all the shit that doesn't
even matter anymore?
Can't we just close the door?
Does it help?
To lock it, bolt it,
reinforce it with armed
guards and VCRs and lipo-
suction and cost reduction
and all the seduction your
memory can muster?
Is it
still too noisy in here?
Out there, is that the smell
of blood and fire in the air?
Has the star that
led us here disappeared
over the horizon, while we're
still waiting for some-
thing else to happen, as if

we hadn't had enough already?
Haven't I too felt like beating or bombing someone
who frightened me or pissed me off because of the way
they looked or acted or seem to be?
Can't we all just get along?
Don't you want to believe we can?
But when your friends are turning up with lies
and alibis for all their sadness and depression
and the recession is supposed to be ending
just when your money's running out,
and they keep smoking and slamming
and jabbing themselves with ways to deform
what they can't even accept yet,
what are we doing here anyway?
Am I wrong?
Was I always?
Is it not about healing, but about tearing
each other's eyes out because we don't
see things the same way?
Is it all about blame?
We're all alive and depend on the ocean and trees,

and the air they give us to breathe—so what are we doing?
Going to any lengths to rip each other off
and tear each other down?
Has the smoke gone away, or not,
because it isn't from the flames
but from the fire that only burns
our lungs like marshmallows at the camps
we never went to, too busy getting here,
where there is no air we can't see,
and the fee for being cynical, like I'm feeling tonight,
is to get up tomorrow and fight my way into a breath
I can remember before this war on all our simple
dreams of harmony got started?
Aren't you feeling brokenhearted too these days?
But not like you lost a lover,
like you're losing the sustainers of your soul and very breath?
Can't we do something about it?
Can't we all just get along—
as in people and trees and animals and seas
and the breeze that will someday stop if we
don't start letting it all go—or never stop—

the hurt and the hate and the need to forget it
with stuff that just adds to the noise and pollution?
Isn't there only one life and one problem and one solution
from the streets to the elite?
Don't we all have a seat
in this universe we share?
Is ours now at the feet
of the oil oligarchy running
what once was our home?
You call this a poem?
Didn't they
used to say
"the best things in life are free"
when they meant
the air and the trees and the sea?
But we know
better now, don't we?
When death is no longer imaginary,
doesn't it all seem like poetry?
Or—is that just me?

Michael Lally's poem "March 18, 2003" was written for and first read at VERSUS: Poets Against The War, a reading which took place at the Paula Cooper Gallery, New York City, on March 18, 2003. The other readers were poets Ann Lauterbach, Anne Waldman, and Robert Creeley. The former United States Attorney General Ramsay Clark also spoke.

The first publication of "March 18, 2003" was in May, 2004, by Libellum books, New York.

Michael Lally

Born in Orange NJ in 1942. First read poetry in coffee houses in late 1950s, first published in 1960, appearing regularly in little magazines after 1966. Attended U. of Iowa Writers Workshop on the GI Bill, in late 1960s, after four years in the Air Force as an enlisted man. While there ran for sheriff of Johnson County, Iowa, on the Peace and Freedom ticket in 1968, coming in a solid second. First book, *What Withers*, published by Doones Press in 1970, twenty-seventh book, *March 18, 2003*, published by Libellum in 2004. Awards include the 1972 92nd St. Y Poetry Center's Discovery Award for *The South Orange Sonnets*; two National Endowment for the Arts Poetry Awards, in 1974 and 1981 (the latter used in attempt to close down the NEA by right-wing Congressmen who accused it of rewarding "pornography" citing the poem *My Life* as an example); 1997 PEN Oakland Josephine Miles Award for Excellence in Literature for *Cant Be Wrong* (Coffee House Press); 2000 American Book Award for *It's Not Nostalgia* (Black Sparrow Press). Meanwhile, worked at variety of jobs, from editor to jazz pianist, hospital night guard to college teacher, chauffer to book critic, (actually in reverse order for all six), and actor (e.g. "Sykes" in the film *White Fang*; the voice of "Sparks" in Ralph Bakshi's *Cool World*; an artist witness on *NYPD Blue*; psychotic detective on *JAG*; crusty Cavalry Captain on *Deadwood*) and script doctor/screenwriter (e.g. wrote narration for *Drugstore Cowboy*; co-wrote with director Ate de Jong the screenplay for *Fogbound*, winner Best Feature Film at the 2003 Thessalaski International Film Festival). Back living in Jersey after forty years elsewhere.

Alex Katz

Alex Katz has collaborated with numerous contemporary poets, including John Ashbery, Robert Creeley, Kenneth Koch, Carter Ratcliff, and has done portraits of many more—Ted Berrigan, Bill Berkson, Edwin Denby, Dick Gallup, Allen Ginsberg, Ann Lauterbach, Alice Notley, Frank O'Hara, Ron Padgett, James Schuyler, Anne Waldman, Lewis Warsh. Katz has had museum exhibitions in Argentina, England, Germany, Ireland, Italy, Spain, and in many institutions in the United States, including the Whitney Museum of American Art. His books include *Alex Katz* (2006, Phaidon), *Alex Katz: The Sixties* (2006, Charta), and *Invented Symbols*, a book of his art education memoirs.

All drawings in the book were made by Alex Katz;
the one on page 41 in 2004, the others in 2006.

Vincent Katz

Vincent Katz is a poet, translator, art critic, editor, and curator. He is the author of nine books of poetry, including *Cabal of Zealots* (Hanuman Books), *Understanding Objects* (Hard Press), and *Rapid Departures* (Ateliê Editorial). He won the 2005 National Translation Award for his book of translations from Latin, *The Complete Elegies of Sextus Propertius* (Princeton University Press). He was awarded a Rome Prize Fellowship in Literature at the American Academy in Rome for 2001–2002 and was a Guest of the Director at the American Academy in Berlin in spring 2006. Katz has written extensively on contemporary art, publishing essays on the work of Francesco Clemente, Jim Dine, Kiki Smith, Philip Taaffe, and Cy Twombly, among others. Katz curated an exhibition on Black Mountain College and edited the catalogue *Black Mountain College: Experiment In Art* (MIT Press). He is the editor of the poetry and arts journal VANITAS and of Libellum books, which first published Michael Lally's "March 18, 2003" in 2004.

Contents

Design
Daniela Meda

Editor
Vincent Katz

Editorial Coordination
Filomena Moscatelli

Copy Editing
Charles Gute

Copywriting and Press Office
Silvia Palombi Arte&Mostre, Milano

Web Design and Online Promotion
Barbara Bonacina

ISBN 88-8158-602-9

Libellum
211 West 19th Street, #5
New York, NY 10011
Tel. +1-212-463-7598
e-mail: libellum@el.net
www.vanitasmagazine.com
www.vincentkatz.com

Edizioni Charta
via della Moscova, 27
20121 Milano
Tel. +39-026598098/026598200
Fax +39-026598577
e-mail: edcharta@tin.it
www.chartaartbooks.it

Printed in Italy

To find out more about Charta, and to learn
about our most recent publications, visit
www.chartaartbooks.it

Printed in May 2006
by Leva, Sesto San Giovanni
for Edizioni Charta